AERO ENGINES
and Other High-Precision Tech

Co-published by agreement between Shi Tu Hui and World Book, Inc.

Shi Tu Hui
Room 1807, Block 1,
#3 West Dawang Road
Chaoyang District, Beijing 100025
P.R. China

World Book, Inc.
180 North LaSalle Street
Suite 900
Chicago, Illinois 60601
USA

Copyright © 2024. All rights reserved. This volume may not be reproduced in whole or in part in any form without prior written permission from the publishers.

WORLD BOOK and the GLOBE DEVICE are registered trademarks or trademarks of World Book, Inc.

Library of Congress Cataloging-in-Publication Data for this volume has been applied for.

Cool Tech (set, hardcover)
ISBN: 978-0-7166-5479-7

Aero Engines and Other High Precision Tech
ISBN: 978-0-7166-5480-3 (hardcover)
ISBN: 978-0-7166-5492-6 (softcover)
ISBN: 978-0-7166-5486-5 (e-book)

Written by Tom Jackson

STAFF

VP, Editorial: Tom Evans
Manager, New Product: Nicholas Kilzer
Curriculum Designer: Caroline Davidson
Proofreader: Nathalie Strassheim
Coordinator, Design Development & Production: Brenda Tropinski
Digital Asset Specialist: Rosalia Bledsoe

Developed with World Book by
White-Thomson Publishing LTD
www.wtpub.co.uk

ACKNOWLEDGMENTS

Cover	© Chesky/Shutterstock
5	© Rolls-Royce
6-7	© Pratt & Whitney
8-9	© leolintang/Shutterstock; © Wirestock Creators/Shutterstock; © Rolls-Royce
10-11	© Marc Ward, Shutterstock; © Rolls-Royce; © GE Aerospace
12-13	© Steffen Weigelt, Rolls-Royce; © United Technologies Corporation; © Composite_Carbonman/Shutterstock; © Maniock/Shutterstock
14-15	© Rolls-Royce; © ararat1980/Shutterstock; © Abaca Press/Alamy Images
16-17	© Rolls-Royce; © Ruben Earth, Getty Images; © luchschenF/Shutterstock; © AP Photo
18-19	© Reaction Engines; NASA/JPL-Caltech; Reaction Engines/ESA
20-21	© Solar Impulse; © Airbus; © John M. Dibbs, Rolls-Royce
22-23	© Fasttailwind/Shutterstock; © N_Sakarin/Shutterstock
24-25	© Antony Souter, Alamy Images; © Pattanapong C, Shutterstock; © photoslick/Alamy Images; © AP Photo
26-27	© Creative Stock Studio/Shutterstock; © Universal Images Group North America LLC/Alamy Images; © Panlop/Shutterstock; © luchschen/Adobe Stock
28-31	© Shutterstock
32-33	© Peter Wollinga, Shutterstock; NASA; Christopher Carranza, U.S. Army Corps of Engineers
34-35	© Budimir Jevtic, Adobe Stock; NASA/CXC/Villanova University/J. Neilsen; © Westend61 GmbH/Alamy Images; Christopher Carranza, U.S. Army Corps of Engineers
36-37	© Shutterstock
38-39	© Warut Pothikit, Shutterstock; © IM Imagery/Shutterstock; © Anatoly/Adobe Stock; © RGB Ventures/SuperStock/Alamy Images
40-41	© Forance/Shutterstock; © agefotostock /Alamy Images; © FocusEurope/Alamy Images; © Science Picture Co/Alamy Images
42-43	© ATLAS Experiment/CERN; © PersimmonPictures.com/Alamy Images
44-45	© Judita Jurkenaite, Shutterstock; © Grandbrothers/Shutterstock; © agefotostock /Alamy Images; © dpa picture alliance/Alamy Images; © Universal Images Group North America LLC/Alamy Images

CONTENTS

Acknowledgments...................................2

Glossary..4

Introduction......................................5

① Aero Engines...................................6

② Testing Technology............................22

③ Remote Sensing................................28

④ Precision Manufacturing.......................36

Resources..46

Index..48

There is a glossary of terms on the first page. Terms defined in the glossary are in boldface type **that looks like this** on their first appearance in the book.

GLOSSARY

avionics the electrical and electronic devices used in aviation (powered flight).

fossil fuel a source of energy that formed from the remains of living things that died millions of years ago. Coal, oil, and natural gas are fossil fuels.

greenhouse gas a gas that warms the atmosphere by trapping heat of solar radiation reflected from Earth's surface, much like the glass in a greenhouse.

hybrid refers to technology that combines two or more existing technologies to perform a function better.

lithography a printing process used to etch patterns on a surface.

microwave a short wavelength radio wave. It varies from 1 to 300 millimeters (about 1/25 to 12 inches) in length. Like light waves, microwaves may be reflected and concentrated. They pass easily through rain, smoke, and fog, which block visible light waves.

nanoscale concerns objects with dimensions between 1 and 100 nanometers. A nanometer is 0.000000001 meter. Nanoscale materials, and the objects made from them, display fundamentally different properties and behavior than the same materials at larger scales.

photolithography a technique in which light is used to etch or imprint the pathways for circuits to follow on a silicon chip. Photolithography is used to produce computer chips.

plasma in physics, this is a form of matter composed of electrically charged particles. The sun and the other stars consist of plasma. Lightning bolts also consist of plasma, but few other plasmas occur naturally on Earth.

remote sensing a technique used to gather information about an object from a distance without actually touching it.

solar panel a panel designed to absorb the sun's rays as a source of energy for generating electricity or heating.

spectrum a range of similar things. The electromagnetic spectrum charts the continuous spread of all types of electromagnetic waves. Light consists of electromagnetic waves. The colors of the rainbow form a spectrum of visible light. The full electromagnetic spectrum also includes forms of energy that cannot be seen by the human eye. These invisible electromagnetic waves include radio waves and X rays.

standard an established point of reference to which other items may be compared.

sustainable practices that can continue to be used over the long term without exhausting resources, damaging the environment, or harming people.

turbine a machine for producing power, in which a wheel or rotor is made to revolve by a fast-moving flow of air, gas, or water.

wavelength the distance between one peak or crest of a wave of light or other electromagnetic energy, and the next corresponding peak or crest. The wavelengths of radio waves are measured in meters; the wavelengths of X rays are measured in billionths of an inch.

INTRODUCTION

Our modern society relies on complex machines and sophisticated technology, such as aircraft engines, satellite sensors, **nanoscale** devices, and computer microchips. These items must be engineered with incredible levels of precision. This not only ensures that they work the first time they are used, but that they are safe and do their job for a long time—often many years—without major repairs. Developing new techniques of precision manufacturing means that modern equipment is much more efficient than in the past. It is important that energy is not wasted as they are being made or used. For example, high-performance aircraft engines can carry large payloads at great speeds over longer distances but are lighter and use less fuel compared to older engine designs.

Another important part of precision manufacturing is the development of new materials. These are often complex mixtures called composites. Composite materials match traditional materials, such as metals, for strength and toughness but are lighter and easier to work with. Precision manufacturing goes hand in hand with an improved ability to measure and test ever more accurately. This ensures that manufacturing processes are meeting design requirements. These technologies used in factories are also used in other applications that benefit from advances in precision. These include mapping, **remote sensing,** and supersensitive instruments used to image the most exotic objects in the universe.

1 AERO ENGINES

JET POWER AND BEYOND

Every year, 4.5 billion people take a flight on a jet-powered aircraft, and around 60 million tons of cargo travels across the world by air. Air travel uses more fuel than any other mode of transportation. Of course, air transportation is much faster, but it uses 100 times as much energy as shipping and is 30 times more energy intensive than a freight train. Modern life is impossible without air travel. But the aircraft industry is a significant source of **greenhouse gases,** which contribute to climate change. To combat climate change, aircraft and aircraft engines must be lighter and more energy-efficient. This efficiency is achieved through new high-tech materials, fuels, and improved engine designs.

ENGINE DESIGNS

The jet engine has been around for more than 75 years, and while the basic idea has not changed, there have been many improvements in its design. In a jet engine, fast-moving air and fuel burn to spin a fanlike system called a **turbine.** The blast of exhaust gases firing backward creates the thrust force, which pushes the whole aircraft forward through the air.

Turbojet. The simplest form of jet engine is the turbojet. This design also produces the most thrust, and so it is used in the fastest jet aircraft, such as supersonic fighters. The turbojet engine has three parts: a compressor, a combustion chamber, and a turbine. As the jet moves through the air, it flows in through the front of the engine into the compressor. This has spinning fan blades that compress (squeeze) the air, making it hotter. The hot air flows into the combustion chamber where it is mixed with a spray of liquid fuel. This mixture explodes, creating hot, fast-flowing exhaust gases. The exhaust blasts out of the back of the engine through the turbine. The flow of gas makes the turbine spin. This rotation is used to drive the compressor at the other end. The exhaust creates the thrust that powers flight. The exhaust gas may contain minute amounts of unburned fuel. In fighter jets, these are set alight by afterburners, which add an extra push to the thrust force.

Adding a fan. Passenger airliners use a jet engine called a turbofan. It is much the same as a turbojet, but there is a large propellerlike fan at the front. This fan is connected to the turbine by a driveshaft running through the middle of the engine. This also connects to the compressor just behind the fan. The fan spins to draw air into the compressor. It also creates a second fast flow of air that goes around the outside of the engine and joins up with exhaust gases, adding to the thrust. A turbofan is more efficient than a turbojet, but it cannot drive an aircraft faster than the speed of sound. At an altitude of 40,000 feet (12,000 meters), sound normally travels at about 660 miles (1,062 kilometers) per hour. Modern airliners using turboprop engines have a top speed of about 650 miles per hour (1,046 kilometers per hour).

Propellers and rotors. Large propeller planes and helicopters also use jet engines. However, in these engines, the energy released by the burning fuel is used to create a fast spinning motion instead of a jet of thrust. Fixed-wing propeller aircraft use a design called a turboprop, while the engine in a helicopter is called a turboshaft.

FUTURE DESIGNS

Turbojet and turbofan designs have steadily improved since the jet engine became the **standard** engine for large aircraft in the 1960's. And the designs are still improving today. For example, larger turbofans are more fuel-efficient. Other new designs completely rethink the function of the fan in a jet engine. Today, high-speed aircraft designers are looking at the scramjet, which utilizes design ideas from rocket engines.

Hypersonic jet. An aircraft that can travel faster than sound is called supersonic. Most military fighter jets are supersonic, but most passenger airliners are not. Aircraft that travel at more than five times the speed of sound are not just supersonic—they are hypersonic. Hypersonic aircraft don't carry human crews. They are used as missiles. The engine on a hypersonic craft is a *scramjet,* short for *supersonic combustion ramjet.* A ramjet is a simple jet engine that has no compressor or turbine. It produces thrust just by burning fuel and only works if it is already moving through the air very fast. In a scramjet, fuel combustion takes place at supersonic air velocities through the engine.

Geared turbofan. A larger turbofan allows it to grab more air to drive through a jet engine and create more thrust. However, a large fan rotates more slowly, so it is attached to the jet engine by the transmission. The gears allow the compressor and turbine to spin very fast and transmit their power to the slower fan. The largest turbofan ever made, the UltraFan by Rolls-Royce, has a fan 12 feet (3.7 meters) wide and has 18 blades. The engine is 10 percent more efficient than older engines. The high-speed turbines generate incredible temperatures inside the engine, so they must be made of high-tech materials that can withstand the heat.

Open rotor. Traditional turbofan designs have the engine fan encased in a streamlined covering called a nacelle. In an open rotor design (also called a propfan engine), the propellerlike fan is left uncovered. An uncovered fan can be made much larger to create more thrust compared to a covered fan engine. The rest of the engine behind the fan also produces thrust to help drive an aircraft forward. The propfan engine has fixed blades behind the propeller. These work to mix the airflow from the propellers. Propfans are efficient and quiet, and so they are popular for smaller aircraft.

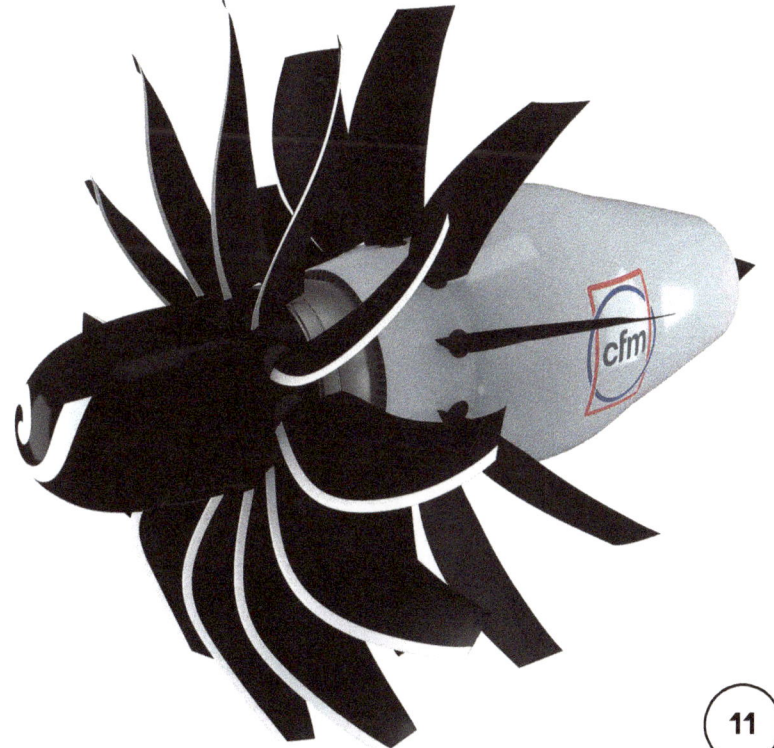

MATERIALS AND MANUFACTURE

Aero engines require precision-built moving parts. The essential parts of a jet engine must be precisely shaped to allow superhot air and gases to flow smoothly. In the extreme environment of a jet engine, there is no room for error! Early jet engine turbine blades were molded from strong metals that made the engine very heavy. Today, new jet engines use novel materials and designs to cut weight and save fuel while maintaining strength.

Composite materials. The new materials used in modern aero engines are called composites. They are a complex mixture of materials including plastics, carbon fibers, and ceramics. These materials can be woven together or built up in layers. The layers are fused into a single composite material using different techniques. They may be baked or locked together with powerful glue.

Modern jet engine nacelles and fan blades are made from composite materials. These materials are designed to match or exceed the properties of the metals used in older designs. The composites do not burn or melt at high temperatures. They do not break easily, but they can bend. Metal must be bent and shaped while hot. But the new composite materials are easily molded into shape. Composite materials make jet engines and aircraft lighter. That means less fuel is needed for each flight. Today's lightweight airliners use about a third less fuel than the all-metal jet aircraft from 40 years ago.

Superalloys. Some components of a jet engine, such as the turbine and compressor, are still made from metal. But modern hollow designs make them lighter while cross supports add strength. The blades must be precisely shaped so they work together efficiently. To shape the blades while maintaining strength, modern turbine blades are made—or perhaps grown—from a superalloy. An alloy is a mixture of different metals—each one adding a useful property. Aircraft bodies and wings use alloys made from lightweight aluminum and titanium, which adds strength. New superalloys used in jet engines also contain nickel. The properties of nickel allow metal components to be constructed, or "grown," from a single crystal. This is achieved by finely controlled cooling of the hot liquid alloy. Since the component is grown from a single metal crystal, there are no microscopic cracks in the engine blade where it might break. The superalloy is strong, so less must be used to make the jet engine components. This reduces the overall weight of the engine and aircraft.

Thermal barrier. Modern high-tech turbine blades are coated in a thin layer of ceramic to protect them from the extreme heat generated inside a jet engine. Tiny holes in the turbine blades allow cold air pumped in from the front to flow through and cool the engine.

GOING WITH THE FLOW

The fan and turbine blades in an aero engine have two jobs. First, they catch the flow of air and harness the energy to turn the linear (straight-line) flow into rotational motion or spin. Next, the blades transfer the rotational motion of the engine to create a linear jet of thrust. The curved shape of the turbine blades helps to do this. Aircraft engineers test their curved blade designs in a wind tunnel to determine which designs work best.

Wide chord. Modern turbofan engine blades have a wide-chord shape. They look like curved swords and have a twisted shape. The chord is the straight line from the front edge of the blade to the back, or trailing, edge. In older aero engines, the fan blades were made from solid metal. They have a simple, narrow, winglike shape that was very strong but often vibrated at full speed. To cut this vibration, engineers added small fins to the middle of the blade. But these reduce efficiency.

New shape. Wide-chord blades in the latest jet engines are bigger and wider, so each blade pushes more air and does not have vibration problems. Modern jet engines need far fewer blades to do their job. The blades in the latest LEAP engines are made from carbon fiber. This flexible material means the blade untwists and straightens as the aircraft reaches top speeds.

Making wind. A wind tunnel is a tunnel through which an artificial wind blows. The wind creates the conditions of a fast-moving jet aircraft moving through the sky. Smoke and gases are released into the wind tunnel to show the airflow clearly. Engineers at the Massachusetts Institute of Technology (MIT) recently built a new wind tunnel named after the Wright Brothers. The new MIT wind tunnel can create hurricane-strength winds using a fan that is 16 feet (4.9 meters) tall. An even larger wind tunnel is found in southern France. The ONERA S1MA wind tunnel can create supersonic airflow using giant fans powered by water flowing down from a nearby mountain reservoir.

NEW FUELS

Modern aviation fuel is a flammable liquid called kerosene. This fuel is similar to gasoline, but it is much thicker and will only ignite (catch fire) at higher temperatures. When it does burn, kerosene generates more heat than gasoline. Kerosene is a **fossil fuel** that burns and produces carbon dioxide (CO_2) as waste gas. Carbon dioxide is a major greenhouse gas contributing to climate change today, so engineers are looking for cleaner aviation fuels. These new fuels must release enough energy to drive today's high-performance aero engines with less harmful waste.

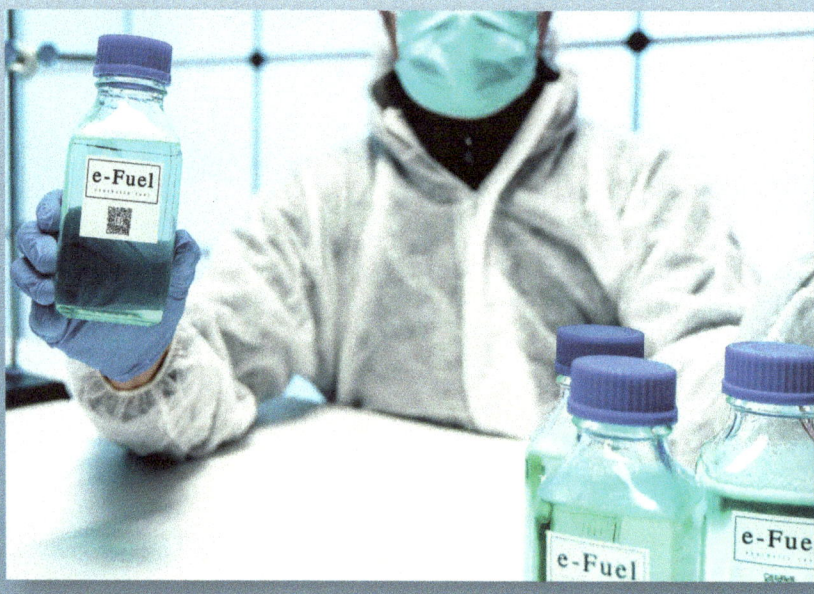

SAF. Clean jet fuel is known as SAF, short for *sustainable aviation fuel*. They are tested using test bed aircraft where an extra engine is attached. SAF's are supposed to be straight swaps for kerosene, meaning that they work in more or less the same way and do not require new jet engine designs to work. Today, most SAF's are biofuels made from plants. Biofuels burn just like kerosene and produce carbon dioxide. However, that carbon dioxide was taken out of the air by the plant from which the fuel was made. Such fuel does not increase the net amount of carbon dioxide in Earth's atmosphere to drive climate change.

Synthetic kerosene. SAF's are made from various raw ingredients. One type, known as HEFA, is made from vegetable oils. A chemical process removes oxygen in the oil to make a thick flammable liquid. HEFA fuels are blended with kerosene to make cleaner jet fuels. However, current production methods struggle to meet the demand for fuel to supply the world's jets. A second, more complicated HEFA production

method uses chemicals from plants and algae to break down the oil to make liquid fuel. This fuel can be produced in larger amounts than the traditional HEFA production system.

Pyrolysis. Wood, nutshells, and other solid ingredients, including food waste and garbage, can be turned into jet fuel by a process called pyrolysis. This process involves slow burning of the material in low oxygen conditions. Pyrolysis produces flammable gases that can then be combined to make liquid jet fuels.

Harnessing the power of hydrogen

Liquid hydrogen. Hydrogen contains three times as much energy as jet fuel and could make a great SAF. Instead of carbon dioxide, hydrogen fuel only produces steam as a waste product. The technological challenge with this fuel is to produce hydrogen in a clean and **sustainable—**or green—way. So far, scientists have not developed cheap, clean, energy-efficient ways to produce hydrogen for fuel. But many people are working to solve that problem. Engineers are already testing jet turbofan engine designs that can use liquid hydrogen as fuel.

POWERING SPACEPLANES

Today's efficient jet engines and the latest aircraft designs mean that passenger jets can fly halfway around the world without landing to refuel. The longest nonstop commercial flights take 20 hours or more—that's a long time to sit on an airplane! Air resistance is an important factor that limits how fast airliners can travel. The air gets in the way. If an airliner could fly over Earth's atmosphere at the edge of space, it could make the same journey in just five hours. To do this, aircraft need a new kind of engine that works in the air and in space.

SABRE. It is impossible to fly to space using a jet engine. There's no air in space, and a jet engine needs a constant flow of air to burn the fuel and produce thrust. Rockets are different. They carry their own supply of oxygen to burn the fuel wherever they are, even in space. The Synergetic Air-Breathing Rocket Engine (SABRE) can switch from a jet engine to a rocket and back again. One day, SABRE engines powered by nonpolluting hydrogen may be used on high-tech airliners that revolutionize travel.

The SABRE engine works like a turbojet that burns hydrogen fuel. It is capable of flying at hypersonic speeds. At these speeds, the air entering the engine is very hot and inefficient for burning hydrogen fuel. Hydrogen fuel can release more energy when it is mixed with colder air. SABRE has a precooling system in front of the engine to solve this problem. The system uses thousands of metal tubes filled with super-cold liquid helium around -420 °F (-250 °C). Air is rapidly chilled as it rushes into the engine between the tubes.

A craft fitted with SABRE engines would take off upright and use its jet engine to blast to 16 miles (25 kilometers) above Earth's surface. At that altitude, the air is too thin for a jet engine to operate. Air intakes close, and the hydrogen fuel is mixed with oxygen from onboard tanks to power the craft as a rocket. Such an aircraft could then fly above the atmosphere at 25 times the speed of sound. When the craft reenters the atmosphere, the air-breathing jet engines engage, and the craft lands at its destination like a typical airliner.

Plasma thruster. Chinese engineers have developed an engine that pushes aircraft using a jet of electrified gas known as **plasma.** A powerful electric current is used to turn air into plasma. Then the plasma is bombarded with **microwaves,** which makes it hot enough to produce a jet of thrust. This may sound like science fiction. But plasma thrust engines may not be so far off in the future.

ALL ELECTRIC

Today, the electric car is replacing gasoline-fueled vehicles. Will the same thing happen with aircraft? Is the future of aero engines electric? That seems unlikely for now. An electric motor creates rotational (spinning) motion, and so can only be used to power propeller engines. Jet engines cannot be directly powered by electricity. Propeller aircraft are smaller, lighter, and slower than jet planes and cannot fly as far. But electric aircraft engine technology is improving.

ACCEL. The current fastest electric airplane is ACCEL (short for ACCeleration of ELectrification of flight) built by Rolls-Royce. The single-seat aircraft has a top speed of 345 miles per hour (556 kilometers per hour). It is powered by the same motors used in electric Formula-E racing cars, and the aircraft's design is a fine balance between the overall weight of the carbon-fiber airframe with the size and power of the batteries and motor carried inside. ACCEL relies on advanced **avionics** to keep it flying. The avionic system uses 20,000 sensors over the aircraft to monitor ACCEL as it flies. An onboard computer automatically adjusts the controls. The aircraft design is pushed to the limit to reach top speed, so a high-tech system is needed.

Hybrid aircraft. The ZEROe is a **hybrid** aero engine system developed by Airbus. It is fueled by hydrogen fuel to power a turboprop engine. However, the hydrogen onboard a ZEROe aircraft can also be used in a fuel cell to make electricity. Inside a fuel cell, hydrogen reacts with oxygen to create a flow of electric current. An onboard motor uses electricity to help spin the engine's propeller and fan, adding an extra boost to thrust when needed. Hybrid aero engines are still being tested. The aim is to have them fitted to aircraft by 2035.

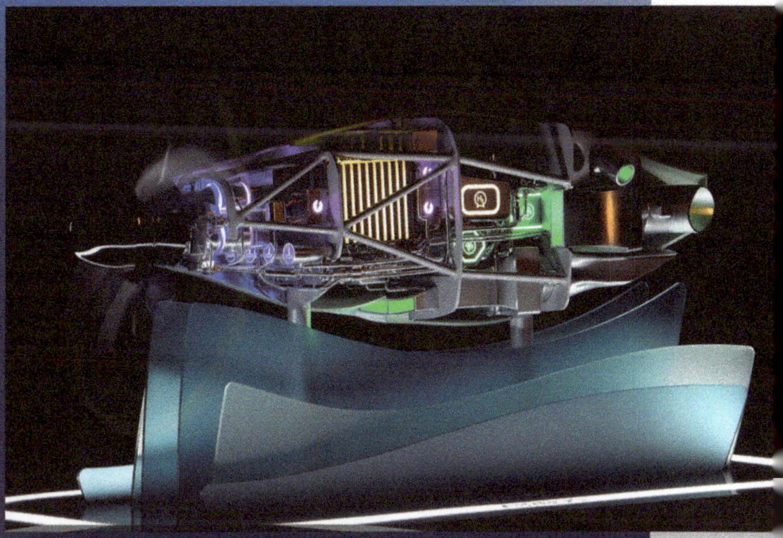

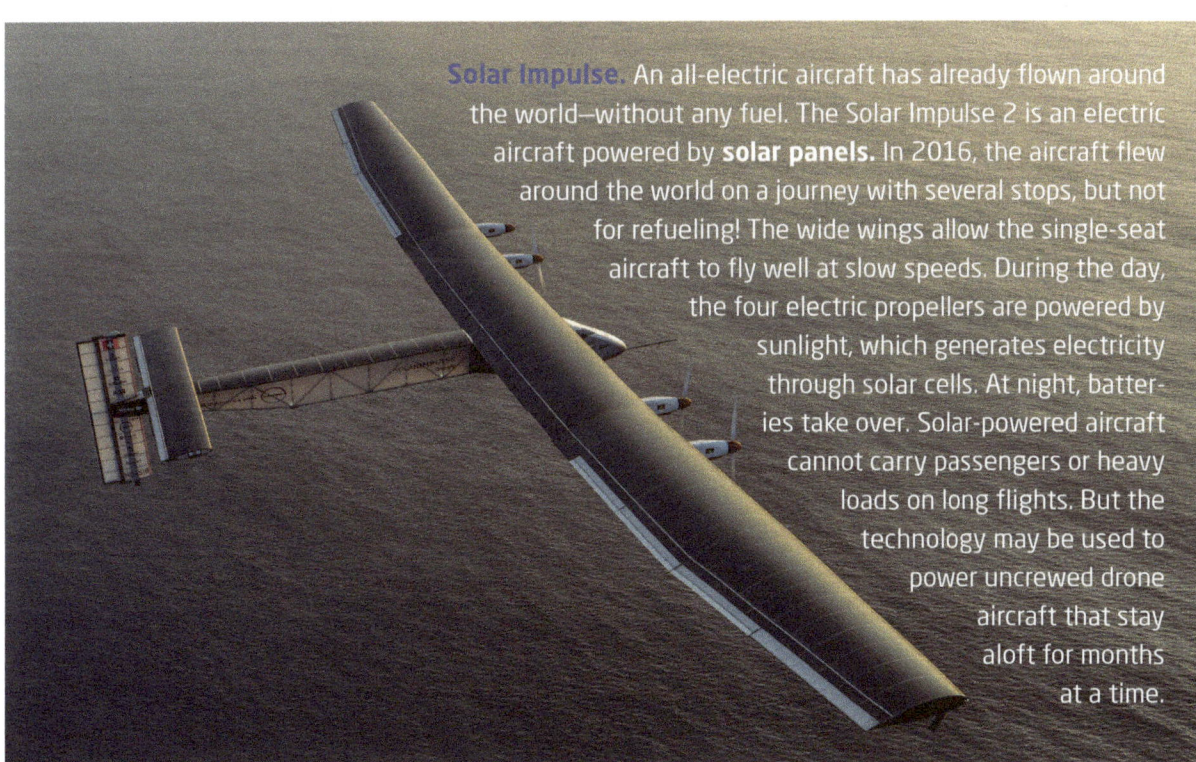

Solar Impulse. An all-electric aircraft has already flown around the world—without any fuel. The Solar Impulse 2 is an electric aircraft powered by **solar panels.** In 2016, the aircraft flew around the world on a journey with several stops, but not for refueling! The wide wings allow the single-seat aircraft to fly well at slow speeds. During the day, the four electric propellers are powered by sunlight, which generates electricity through solar cells. At night, batteries take over. Solar-powered aircraft cannot carry passengers or heavy loads on long flights. But the technology may be used to power uncrewed drone aircraft that stay aloft for months at a time.

2 TESTING TECHNOLOGY

TAKING A GOOD LOOK

Testing is an important factor in precision manufacturing. Precision technology needs to be just right—the right shape, the right strength, or made from the correct materials—otherwise it does not function. One way to check is to take the item apart and take a look inside. However, the item is destroyed in the process, so a set of technologies called nondestructive testing is used. These technologies use a wide variety of engineering methods to get a close-up view of manufactured items inside and out. Such tests are used to check that aircraft and other important machines are undamaged and safe to use. Impurities in materials used in high-tech machines can cause serious problems, so chemical testing is used to check materials used in the manufacturing process.

FINDING FLAWS

The moving parts of an aero engine or other precision machines will eventually need replacing. If they are not replaced in time, an engine part such as a fan blade will break. The broken component may destroy other parts of the engine and could damage the aircraft as a whole. This is not just an expensive failure—it is life-threatening when it happens thousands of feet in the air. Today, aero engines, wings, and other aircraft parts are regularly tested for early signs of wear or cracking using a range of nondestructive techniques.

Eddy currents. Metal objects like turbine blades are tested using an electromagnetic system that relies on induction. Induction is the process where a magnetic field creates an electric current inside a metal conductor. The eddy-current test does this using a probe with an electrified coil inside, which is held near the component to be tested. This creates swirling electric currents—called eddy currents—and a small magnetic field inside the component that is detected by the probe. Tiny cracks in the metal change how the eddy currents appear, and so provide an early warning that a structural problem exists in the component.

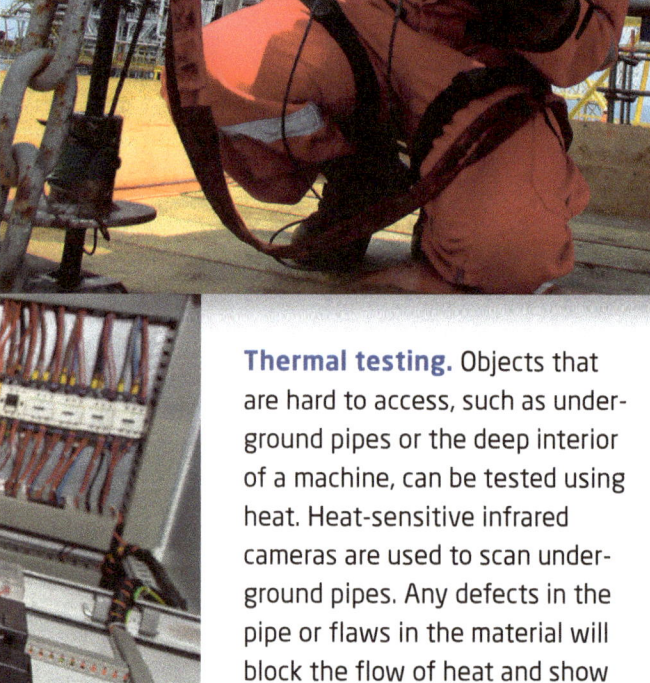

Thermal testing. Objects that are hard to access, such as underground pipes or the deep interior of a machine, can be tested using heat. Heat-sensitive infrared cameras are used to scan underground pipes. Any defects in the pipe or flaws in the material will block the flow of heat and show up as cooler, darker areas on an infrared image.

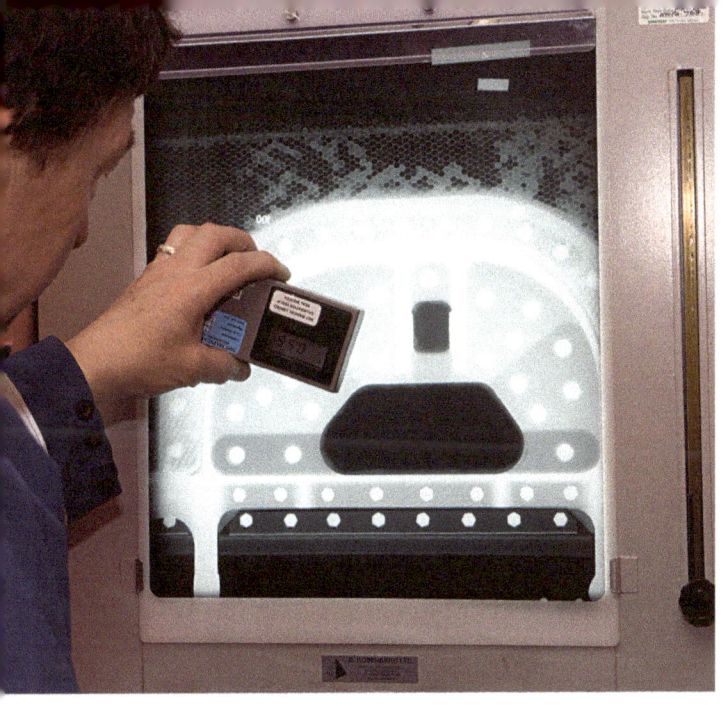

Industrial radiography. Radiography is a common technology in medicine. X ray and Computed Tomography (CT) scans are designed for looking inside the body. The same technology can be used to examine machines and components. Medical scans use high-energy beams like X rays. Medical technicians must be careful to ensure that the beams are not strong enough to damage body tissues. Industrial radiography can use powerful beams of X rays and high-energy gamma rays to penetrate metal and other hard components. Industrial radiography scans are especially good for checking the strength of welded metal and examining layered composite materials.

T-waves. Short for *terahertz waves,* T-waves are invisible beams similar to heat and radio waves. Like X rays, the T-waves can pass through solid objects. But unlike X rays, they do not damage the materials. T-wave body scanners are at airports and other security checks to look for items hidden under clothing. T-waves are good for scanning sensitive nonmetal objects, such as microchips, for defects.

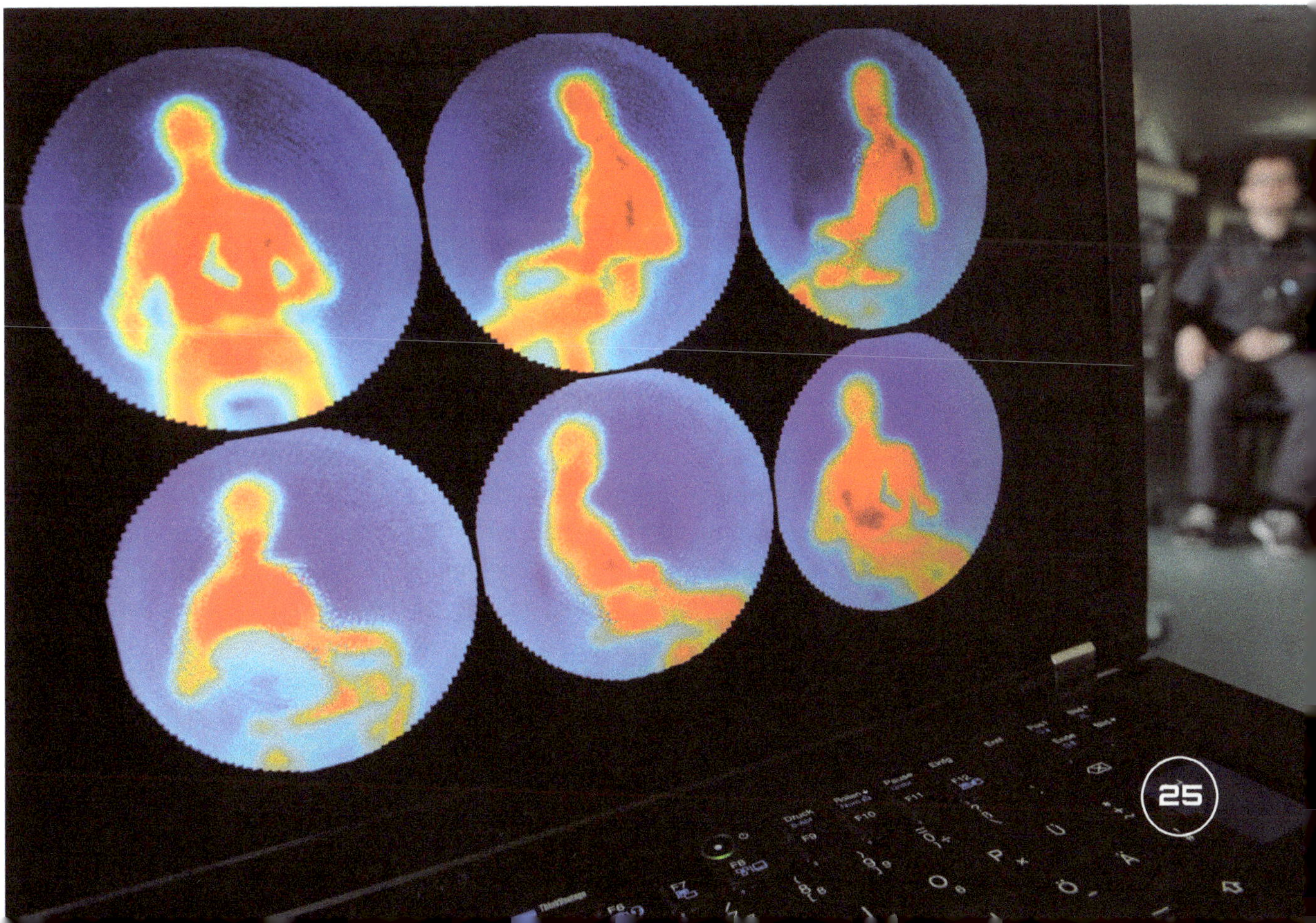

CHEMICAL TESTING

Modern high-tech machines and instruments are rarely constructed from a single material. Instead, the components are made from various materials, such as metal alloys and composites (combined materials). The raw ingredients in these materials must be mixed in precise quantities, and impurities must be removed for the material to perform as expected. Today, a range of chemical testing technologies are used to ensure that only the right substances are used.

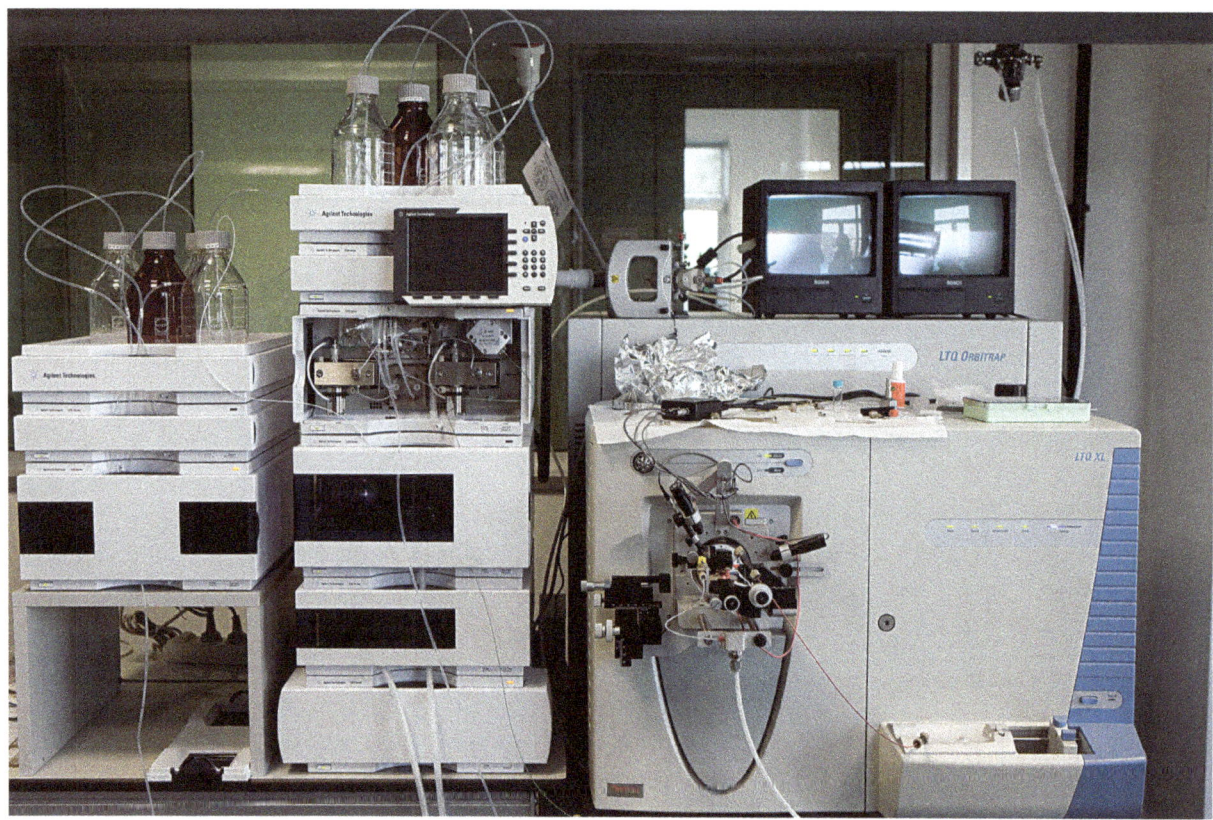

Mass spectrometer. The best way to analyze what substances are in a mixture is to use a mass spectrometer. This is an old piece of technology that was invented around 100 years ago, but back then these devices filled an entire room. Today's mass spectrometers are handheld and can be used anywhere.

A mass spectrometer works by turning a substance into an electrified gas. The gas particles are fired into a vacuum with an electric field running across it. The electric field pushes and pulls on the particles. The smaller particles move farther than the heavier ones, so the particles in the sample become spread out according to their mass, creating a **spectrum.** That spectrum of particles then hits a detector that shows the size and quantity of the different particles. All atoms have a unique mass, so a mass spectrometer can determine what atoms and molecules are in the sample.

Chromatography. This technology is used to separate materials that make up a liquid or gaseous mixture and have similar properties. One use of it is to measure or identify low concentrations of substances, such as pollutants in air or water. Another use is to separate and identify products of chemical reactions. Chemists use this method to separate pure substances from impurities. Chromatographic methods are based mainly on a process called adsorption. A mixture passes through a solid or liquid material that adsorbs (attracts to its surface) substances. Various substances are adsorbed at different rates of speed, so the substances in a mixture separate from one another as the mixture moves through the material.

Gas chromatography pushes gases through a long narrow tube, and the lighter components emerge first and the heavier components later. This kind of testing is used to determine the substances in such complex mixtures as biofuels and natural oils.

Electrophoresis. This kind of chromatography uses an electric current to push molecules through a gel. Smaller molecules move through the gel faster, leaving behind the larger ones. Once the separation is complete, the gel is stained with a dye to reveal the separation bands, which resemble a barcode. It is especially useful for separating delicate biological chemicals like DNA and proteins. Gel electrophoresis is widely used in biology and biochemistry labs and in such fields as forensic science, conserva-

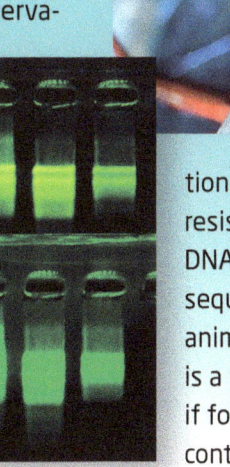

tion biology, and medicine. Electrophoresis is also used in DNA profiling and DNA barcoding. A DNA barcode is a DNA sequence commonly used to identify animals, plants, and microbes. Barcoding is a precision technology that can show if food or other biological products are contaminated.

3 REMOTE SENSING

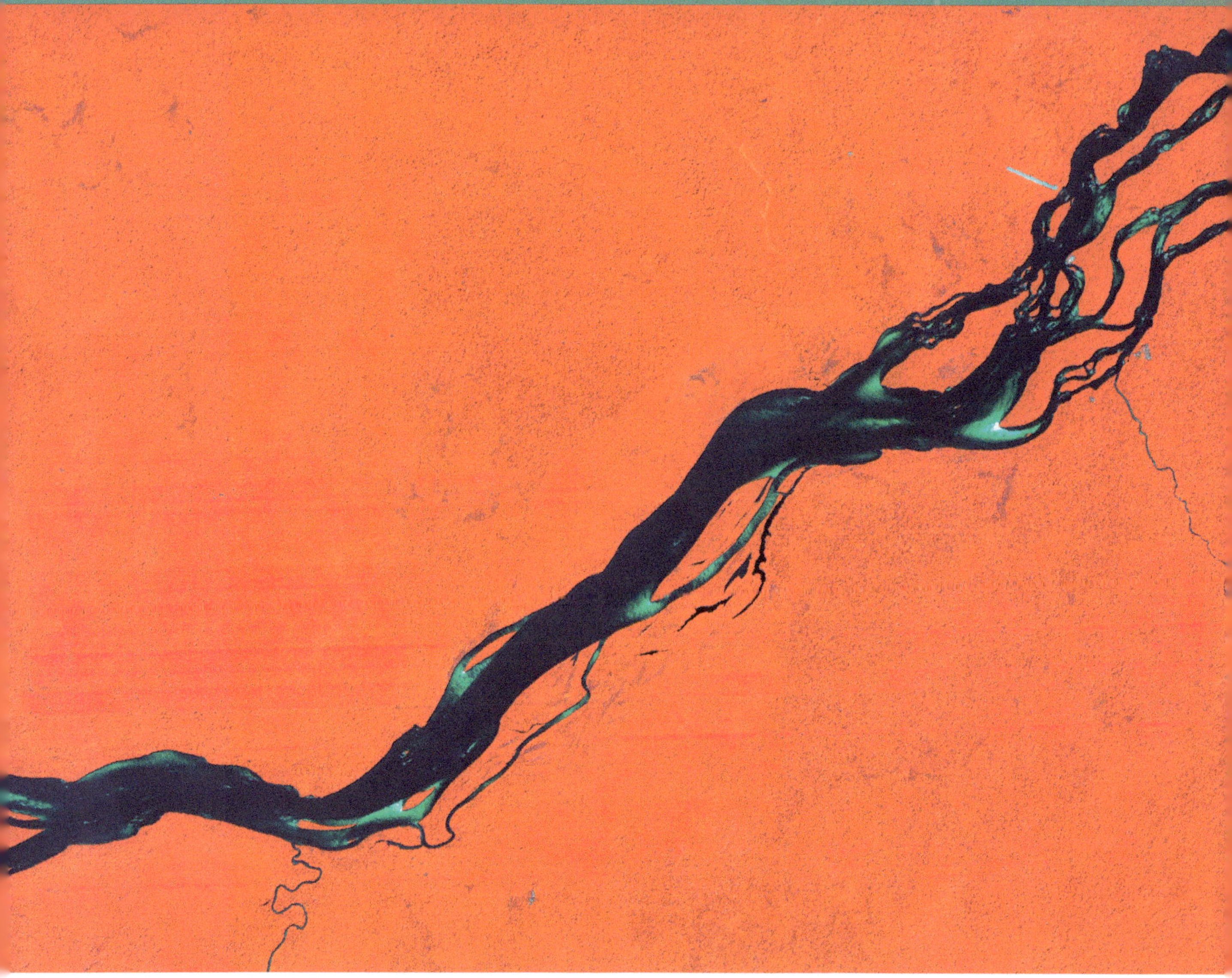

LOOKING FROM AFAR

High-precision tech is helping us learn more about our planet through remote sensing. This technology collects information coming from Earth's surface, which it uses to build better maps, understand climate change, measure polar ice cover, and assess ecological conditions and damage. Remote sensors can monitor disasters, such as wildfires and volcanoes, from a safe distance. Remote sensing is also used in archaeology to discover long-lost cities buried beneath the ground or hidden by jungle overgrowth.

Remote sensing is typically carried out from a high altitude, either using orbiting satellites or aircraft. These are fitted with a range of detectors capable of making precise measurements. Remote sensing satellites usually orbit Earth around the poles. That allows the satellite to pass over and survey all of Earth's surface as the planet spins underneath it. Remote sensing tech uses radio waves, laser beams, and sound pulses to create a detailed picture of the planet.

PASSIVE REMOTE SENSING

Passive remote sensing technology works by collecting the different sources of radiation emitted (given off) or reflected from Earth's surface. Such radiation sources may include a heat plume of an erupting volcano, a flash of lightning, sunlight reflected off Earth's surface, or the lights of a city at night. The kind of radiation measured by remote sensors and the way it varies over Earth indicates the conditions on the surface.

Spectrometer. A spectrometer is an instrument that spreads out light and other types of radiation into a spectrum and displays it for study. Passive radiation sources on Earth are picked up by spectrometers on board satellites and high-flying aircraft. These sensors split the radiation into separate **wavelengths** of visible light and such invisible beams as ultraviolet (UV) and infrared (IR) radiation.

Airborne and satellite-based spectrometers allow materials to be mapped across the landscape. For example, gases absorb and emit specific colors of light. The spectrometer uses this information to show what gases are in Earth's atmosphere. Remote sensing spectrometers are used to map major sources of greenhouse gases, including carbon dioxide and methane, around the globe.

Radiometer. This sensor picks up the intensity of radiation, such as light or UV and IR. One use of radiometers is to measure the location and thickness of clouds and to monitor masses of water vapor as they flow through the atmosphere. This information helps climate scientists. Precipitation radiometers detect rain and snow in clouds and are used to make detailed maps of rain falling over a wide area of the planet.

Lightning imaging sensor. NASA has a satellite orbiting far out in space that is counting lightning strikes on Earth. The Geostationary Lightning Mapper uses cameras to pick up each flash. Unlike many remote sensing satellites, this spacecraft is in a geostationary orbit 22,236 miles (35,786 km) out in space. Geostationary satellites orbit at the same speed as the Earth turns. The satellite always stays above the same point on the surface and can see one-half of the planet all at once.

31

ACTIVE REMOTE SENSING

Active remote sensing systems scan the surface with a beam and detect the signal reflected back. Active systems include radar and lidar, but also sensors called scatterometers and interferometers, which are designed to detect how distant objects and materials alter the original beam. Active sensors can be satellite-based, and they are commonly used in aircraft that can make more detailed surveys of smaller target regions.

Radar is the oldest active remote sensing technology, having been developed in the 1930's. Radar stands for RAdio Detection And Ranging. Radar stations send out a beam of radio waves that reflect off the objects and bounce back. The echoes reveal the shape, size, and location of the object. Modern remote sensing radar often uses microwave beams, which can pass through clouds and the air easily and reflect off objects better than radio waves. The newest radar technology includes four-dimensional (4D) radar. This technology uses echoes and a concept called time-of-flight measurement to map objects in a three-dimensional (3D) environment. It is currently being tested in self-driving automobiles to map items in a vehicle's path. Four-dimensional radar differs from standard radar in that it can detect when a vehicle is moving and determine speed in a wide variety of weather and environmental conditions.

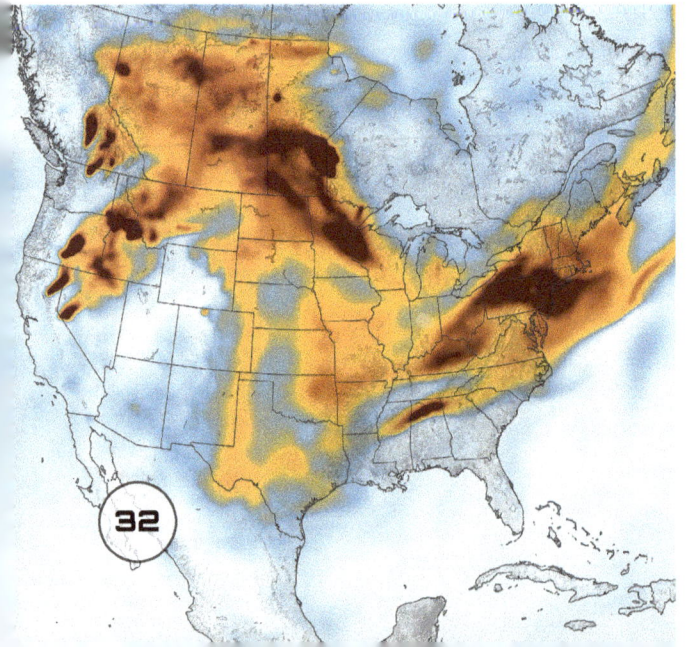

Lidar. Standing for LIght Detection And Ranging, lidar works on a principle similar to that of radar and is sometimes called optical radar or laser radar. Lidar can be used to determine the direction, distance, shape, and speed of objects from a great distance. Lidar is the main technology behind autonomous vehicles and advanced driver assistance systems, and it has many applications in robotics.

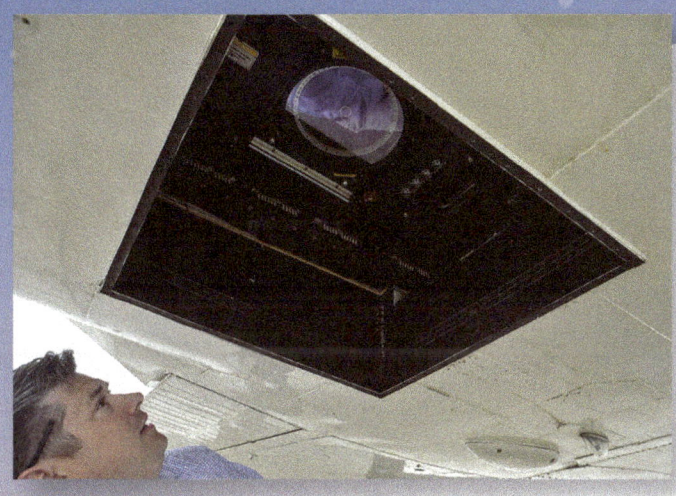

Lidar sensors on aircraft are better for mapping the surface of Earth. In archaeology, Lidar is used to create detailed, high-resolution maps of prehistoric sites and the surrounding landscape in remote regions. Lidar's ability to penetrate vegetation to reveal hidden structures helps archaeologists discover unknown sites that are nearly impossible to detect using conventional methods. Lidar technology can effectively "see through" dense forests, undergrowth, and layers of soil.

Scatterometers. The laser and radar beams sent out by these sensors do not reflect back to create a clear echo. Instead, they are scattered in all directions, and the sensor collects the scattered reflection. Scatterometers attached to the International Space Station are used to detect wind flows in Earth's atmosphere.

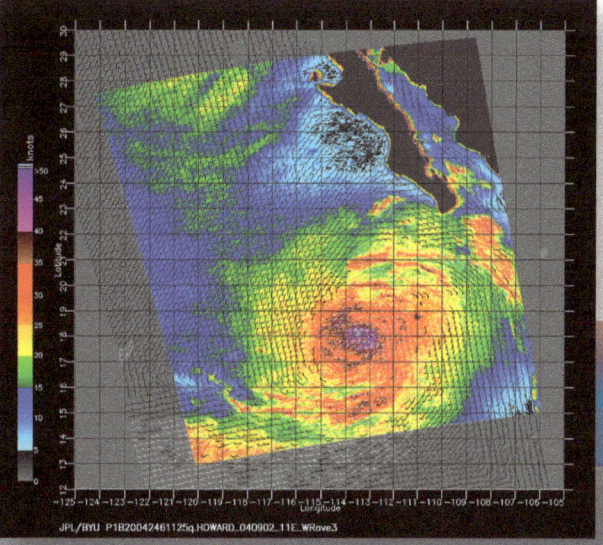

Altimeter. Lasers are useful for measuring distances and are an important part of sensors called altimeters. These measure altitudes and are an important tool in mapping the height of the land above sea level. For the altimeter to work, it needs to know how high it is. It can do this by measuring the distance to a known landmark with verified altitude. One of the best locations is Bolivia's Salar de Uyuni, the world's largest salt flat, which is also the flattest place on Earth.

MAPPING THE OCEAN FLOOR

Most of the ocean floor on Earth is 12,000 feet (3,700 meters) underwater. The scientific measurement of the ocean depths is called bathymetry—a perfect application for remote sensing technology. But many remote sensing technologies, such as radar, are unable to penetrate the water. Maps of Earth's ocean floor today have fewer details than maps of the moon. However, new high-precision tech is helping to steadily create a clear picture of the deep ocean.

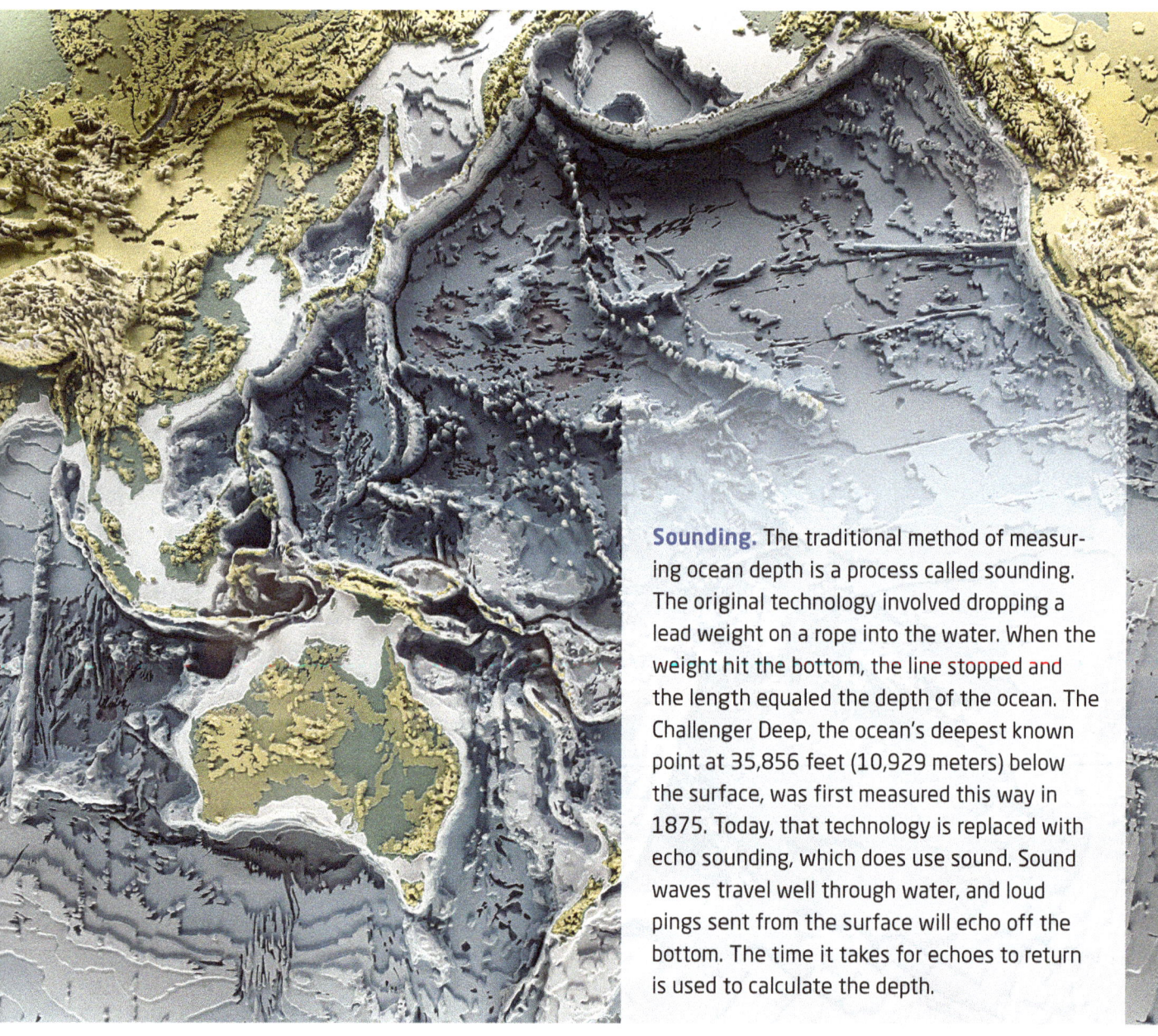

Sounding. The traditional method of measuring ocean depth is a process called sounding. The original technology involved dropping a lead weight on a rope into the water. When the weight hit the bottom, the line stopped and the length equaled the depth of the ocean. The Challenger Deep, the ocean's deepest known point at 35,856 feet (10,929 meters) below the surface, was first measured this way in 1875. Today, that technology is replaced with echo sounding, which does use sound. Sound waves travel well through water, and loud pings sent from the surface will echo off the bottom. The time it takes for echoes to return is used to calculate the depth.

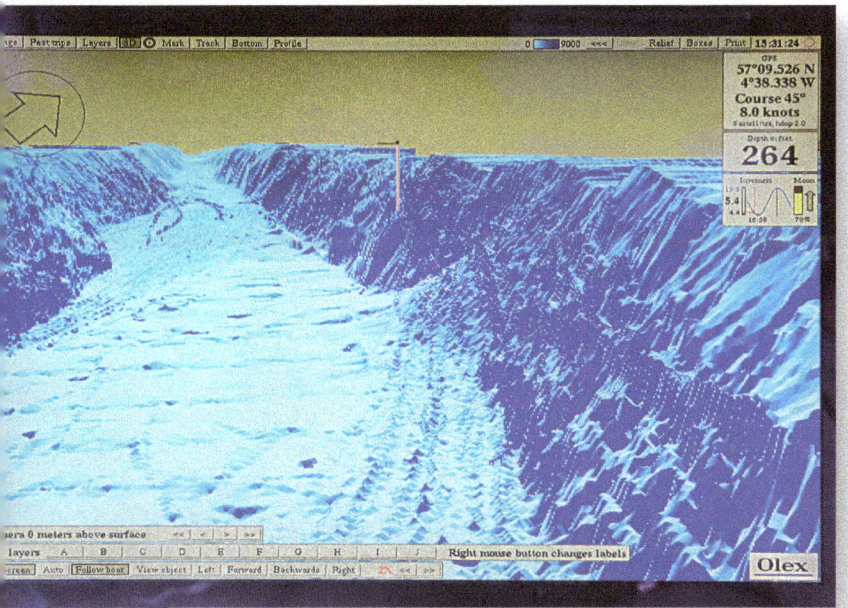

Sonar is a technology that uses sound energy to locate objects; measure their distance, direction, and speed; and even produce pictures of them. The word *sonar* comes from SOund Navigation And Ranging. Sonar is often only able to make fuzzy maps, and the sound beams it uses are often narrow, especially in shallow water. Many important features of the ocean floor have been discovered by sonar and echo sounding. New survey ships with wide-beams sonars are being developed to cover more area. These modern sonar devices are often towed behind a large survey ship.

Lidar bathymetry. A faster way to map the ocean floor is to use airborne lidar. This technology works especially well in shallow water. Lidar is particularly useful for mapping tidal zones along the coast, where the water meets the land. Here, the most detailed maps are needed to ensure the safety of shipping.

Lidar is increasingly used to map deeper parts of Earth's oceans. The Monterey Bay Aquarium Research Institute in California is partnering with a company called 3D at Depth to use its subsea lidar system (SL1) incorporated on a remotely operated vehicle (ROV) to map the ocean floor. The SL1 was originally designed to inspect underwater equipment in the oil and gas industry. In 2017, the two organizations deployed their next-generation Wide Swath Subsea LiDAR (WiSSL) to map the ocean floor with centimeter-scale precision.

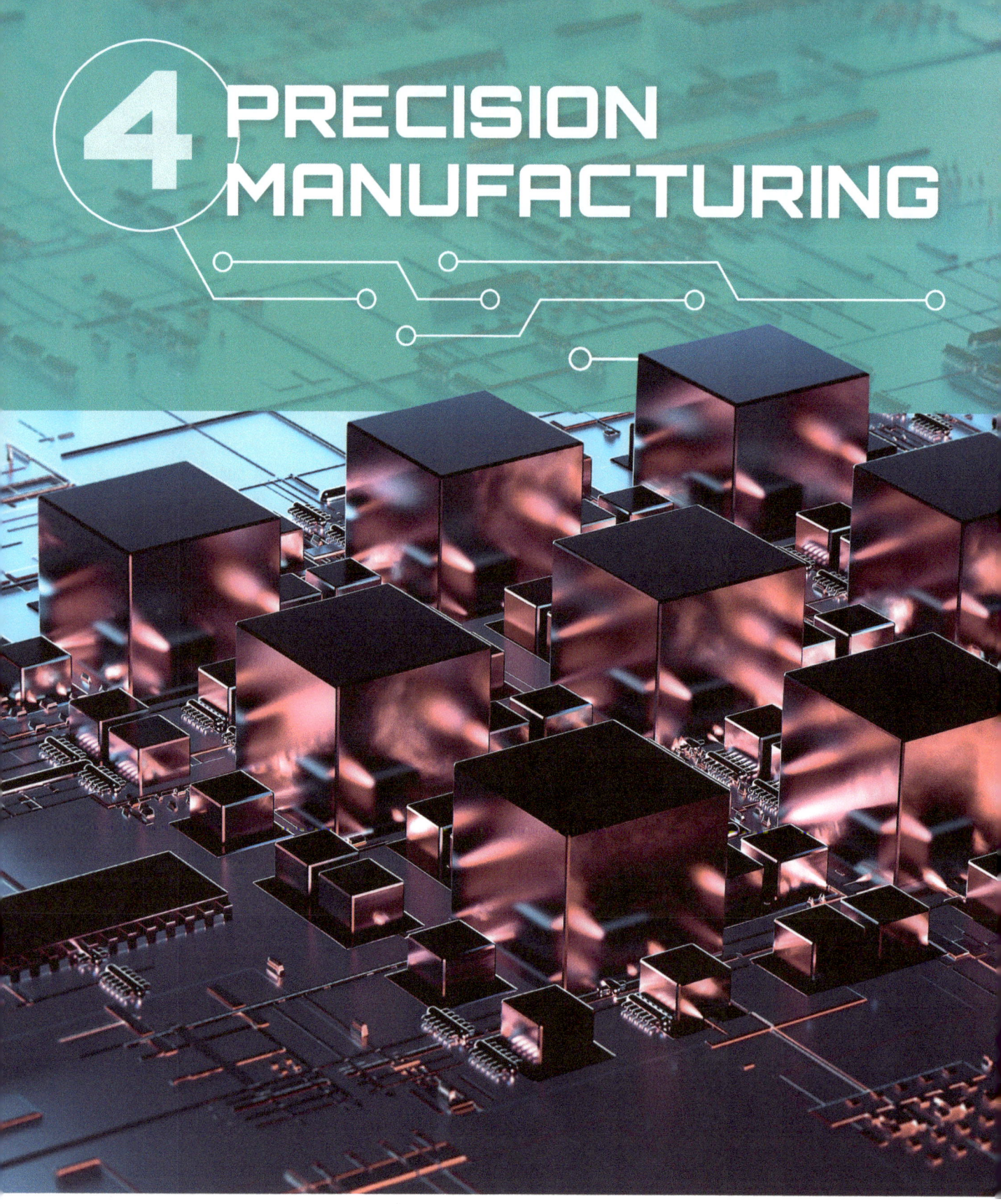
4 PRECISION MANUFACTURING

GETTING IT EXACTLY RIGHT

Modern high-tech manufacturing is getting ever more precise. Factories must produce a continuous supply of complex products that are uniform and identical. There is no room for error when manufacturing high-precision technology components, such as computer microchips and sensitive scientific instruments. Here, components are measured in millionths or billionths of a meter. And cutting-edge technology will be even smaller in the future. Nanotechnology is a new area where entire devices can be built from a handful of atoms. Perhaps the ultimate examples of high-precision technology are the instruments used to make accurate measurements.

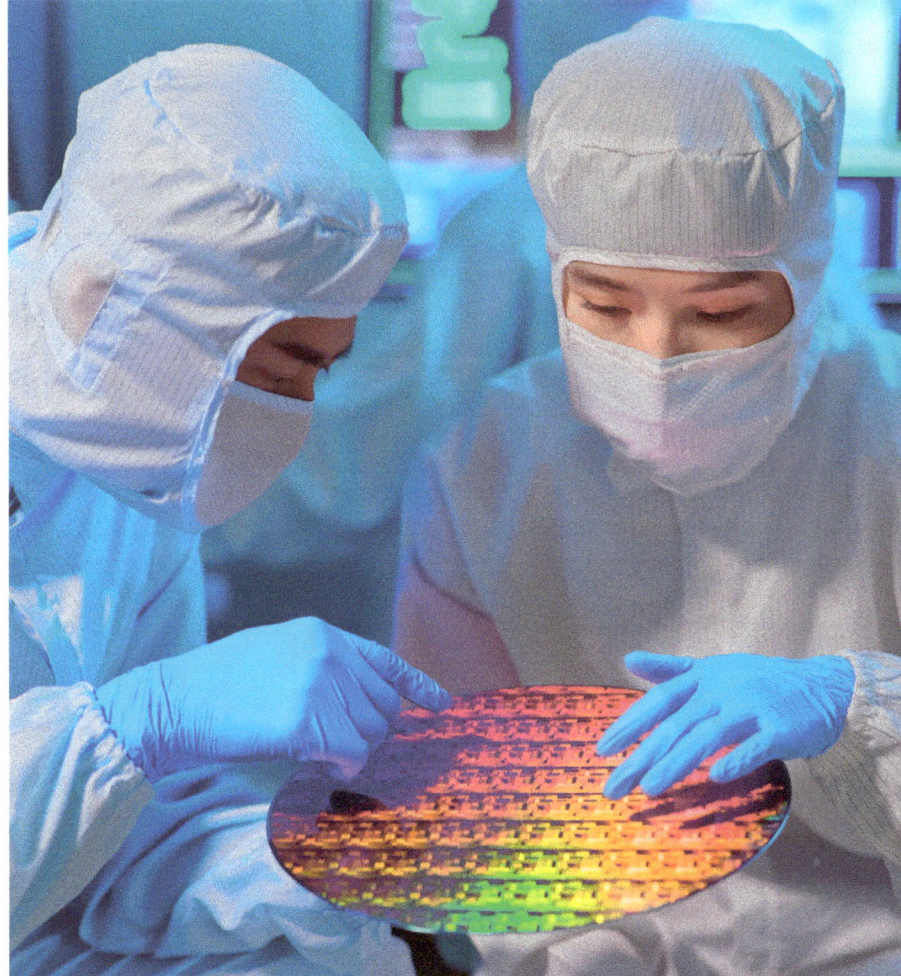

MICROCHIP TECHNOLOGY

A microchip is a piece of pure silicon that has tiny electronic components integrated into it. Depending on how they are arranged, these components will work as a processor for a computer, or they may be used as computer memory. A modern chip about the size of your fingernail may have 60 billion separate components. Each must work and be connected in exactly the right way. For decades, the number of components on computer chips has doubled every two years. That phenomenon—known as Moore's Law—continues today. Today, 100 billion computer chips are working in our devices—and each one is a piece of high-precision tech.

Microfabrication. A microchip factory is often called a fab. The term comes from microfabrication, the process used to make these products. Microfabrication is done using a high-tech process called **photolithography.** This process creates an intricate pattern of tiny components on a blank silicon chip. The process is partly like taking a photograph and partly like printing. To start with, a chip is coated with a light-sensitive chemical called photoresist. Next, the chip is covered with a mask made of glass. The mask is a master copy of the circuit pattern that will be etched on the microchip. The mask is transparent where components will be located on the chip. Blacked-out spaces on the mask represent spaces between components on the chip.

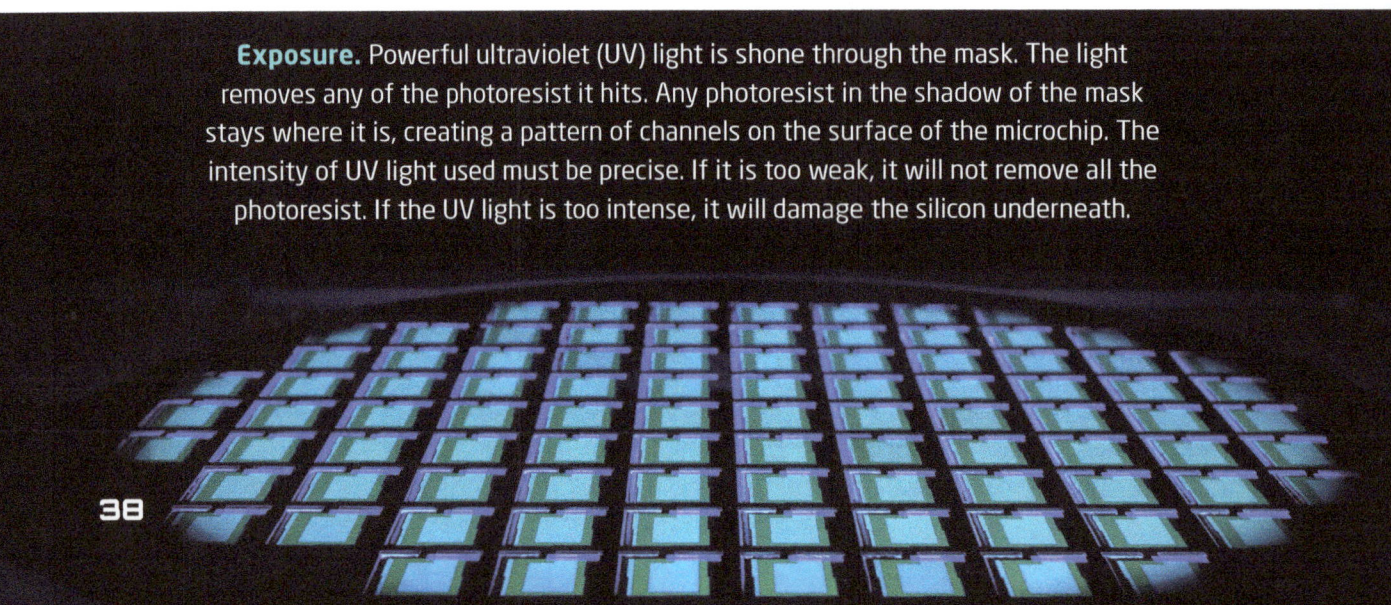

Exposure. Powerful ultraviolet (UV) light is shone through the mask. The light removes any of the photoresist it hits. Any photoresist in the shadow of the mask stays where it is, creating a pattern of channels on the surface of the microchip. The intensity of UV light used must be precise. If it is too weak, it will not remove all the photoresist. If the UV light is too intense, it will damage the silicon underneath.

EUV. The latest photolithography systems use extreme ultraviolet exposure (EUV). EUV uses a narrow beam of UV to make smaller and more precise patterns on the microchip. In 2022, China's Huawei company developed an EUV system to etch components just 3 nanometers across. One nanometer equals one-millionth of a millimeter. With incredibly small components like these, more can be fit on a chip to make computers faster and more powerful.

Doping. Once the chip circuits have been etched onto the silicon, the etching is filled with certain metals and doped to create transistors that control the flow of electric current in the chip. Doping is a process that adds precise levels of such impurities as boron, aluminum, indium, arsenic, or antimony to the pure silicon to alter its electrical properties and create the tiny components of a computer chip.

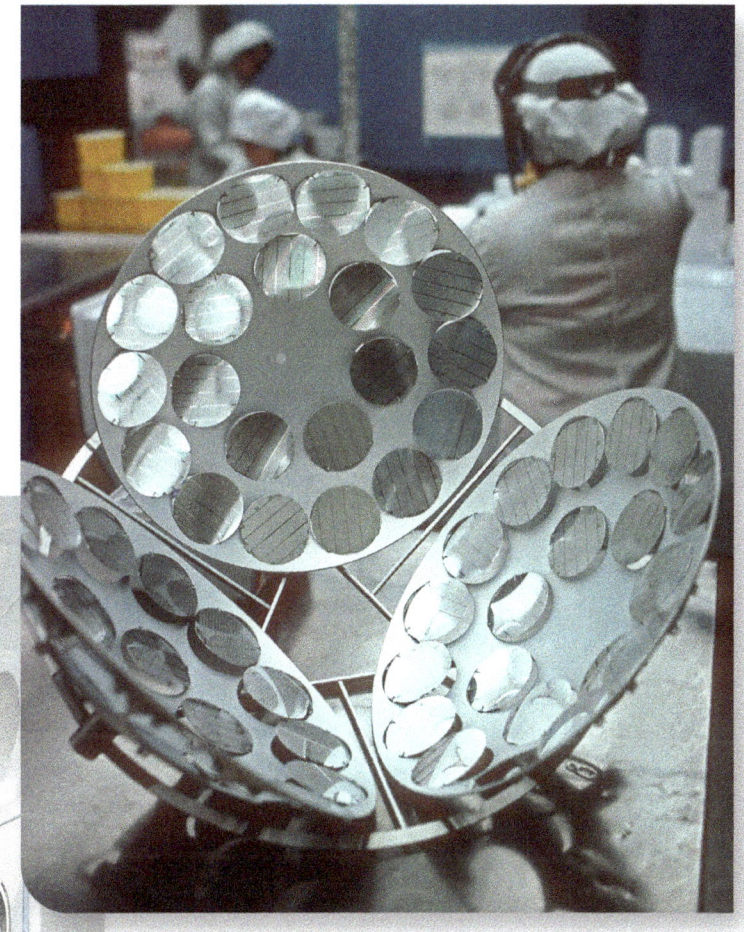

Impurities. With chip components only a few billionths of a meter across, any impurities that contaminate the photolithography process can be disastrous. Modern microchip fabs are typically kept inside clean rooms that use high-tech filters to keep dust and other tiny particles out. These are some of the cleanest places on Earth! To avoid contaminating the microfabrication process, the Intel Corporation uses fab clean rooms that have 1,000 times fewer airborne particles than a hospital operating room.

NANOTECHNOLOGY

Nanotechnology is all about precision. A nanometer is 0.000000001 meter—one-millionth of a millimeter (or one-billionth of a meter). A nanomaterial is anything that is less than 100 nanometers in size. That's 100,000 times smaller than the width of a human hair. Materials this size are already used in everyday applications, such as dyes and skin creams. But in these products, the nanomaterials are just an ingredient in a mixture of chemicals. Scientists and engineers working to build components and entire machines with nanomaterials is a new area of high-precision tech. This means working on the nanoscale.

Today, nanoscale machines are mostly in the experimental stage. The challenges of creating working components for a machine on the nanoscale are impressive. There are two main approaches to creating nanoscale objects: (1) top-down and (2) bottom-up. The top-down approach involves removing material, much as a sculptor does, to produce nanoscale objects. The bottom-up approach involves the use of biological or chemical methods to build structures and devices from atoms or molecules. Scientists first achieved this kind of assembly by using sensitive probes to manipulate individual atoms or molecules—a time-consuming task.

Electron-beam lithography.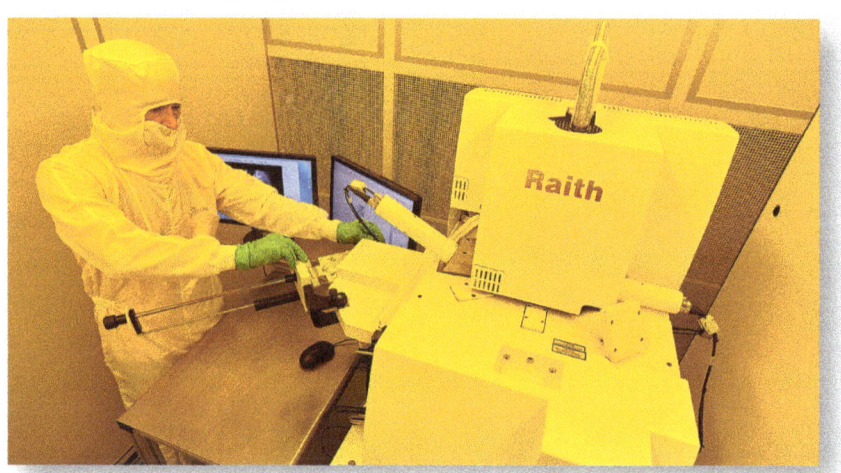
One top-down method, called electron beam **lithography,** uses a beam of electrons to etch patterns on materials coated with an electron beam-sensitive resist. This technology allows microfabrication of computer chips at the nanoscale—far smaller than what can be achieved using photolithography.

Quantum dot. One kind of nanotechnology already used today is called a quantum dot. This is a nanoparticle made of semiconductor materials—a single crystal of silicon about 5 nanometers wide, doped with other substances. Quantum dots have many interesting qualities. For instance, they can store or move electrons and emit light in different colors when they are exposed to UV light. They are used today in televisions. They may also be used in quantum computers where the processing power is billions of times higher than today's desktop computers. Quantum dots could also be an important building block for self-assembled functional nanodevices.

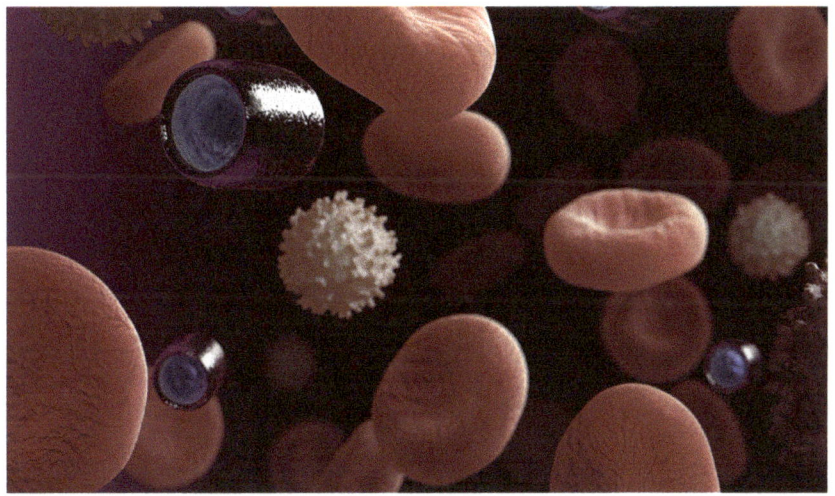

Self-assembly. A bottom-up process called self-assembly may be a more effective method of creating nanoscale objects. Self-assembly is common in nature. It is the process by which, for example, an acorn grows into an oak tree rather than another plant. Organic or biological molecules have the potential to direct the self-assembly of nanostructures.

DNA nanorobots. Nature has already created nanoscale machines in the form of tiny cells, such as bacteria and viruses, and biological molecules like DNA (deoxyribonucleic acid). DNA is a thin, chainlike molecule found in every living cell. It directs the formation, growth, and reproduction of cells and organisms. Instead of trying to create new molecules that function as nanomachines, scientists are working to turn short strands of DNA into chemical nanorobots that can walk, swim, or pick up other molecules. These nature-based nanomachines may one day have many useful functions in medicine and biotechnology.

SCIENTIFIC INSTRUMENTS

High-precision tech is used in all areas of science. Sensitive scientific instruments allow us to see the smallest objects in great detail and look out far into space to see objects billions of light-years away. Such giant machines as particle accelerators, used to investigate the basic properties of matter, also rely on precision measurements and detectors. For astronomers, "seeing" a black hole in space requires modern technology used in novel ways.

Particle detectors. The Large Hadron Collider (LHC) outside Geneva, Switzerland, is the largest and most complex machine ever made. A particle accelerator is a huge device designed to accelerate particles of matter (called hadrons) to extremely high energies and then collide them. By studying the results of the collisions the LHC produces, scientists hope to learn more about the nature and properties of matter. The particles released by LHC collisions are incredibly small—only a few femtometers across (a femtometer is one thousand-trillionths of a meter)—and they exist for only a fraction of a second before they disintegrate.

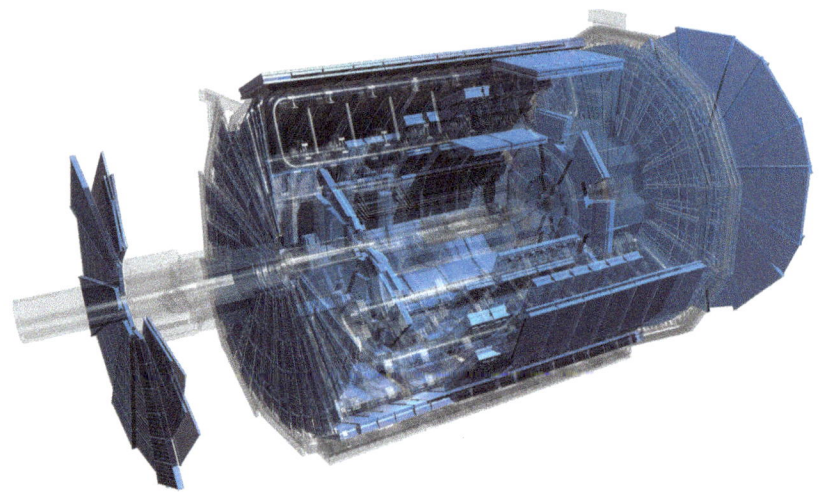

The LHC uses a variety of detectors to record the particles that are produced in collisions. The detectors are designed to measure the energy, momentum (motion), and electrical charge of the particles produced from the collisions. The two main types of detectors used at the LHC are the ATLAS and CMS detectors. ATLAS (short for A Toroidal LHC Apparatus) has more than 100 million sensitive components to record the particles produced by the collisions. Electrically charged particles are steered toward detectors using a series of doughnut-shaped magnets called toroids. The Compact Muon Solenoid (CMS) is a general-purpose detector at LHC. CMS acts as a giant high-speed camera to capture 3D images of particle collisions 40 million times each second.

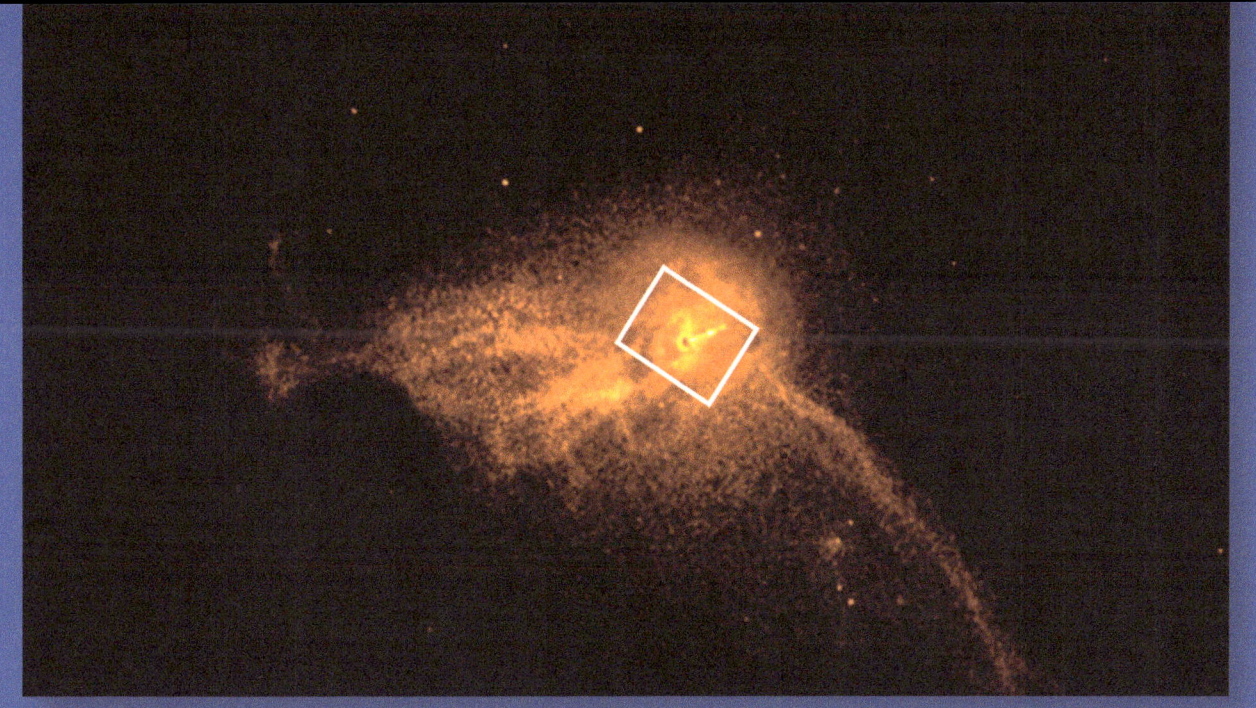

Event Horizon Telescope. Is it possible to "see" a black hole? A black hole is a region of space whose gravitational force is so strong that nothing can escape from it. A black hole is invisible because it even traps light. But in 2019, the Event Horizon Telescope (EHT) managed to take the first picture of a black hole. The EHT is not one piece of tech, but a group of space probes and telescopes that each looked for different wavelengths of X rays and gamma rays coming from a black hole in deep space called M87. This allowed astronomers to make an image of the black hole's shadow against the background of superhot gases that surround it.

MAKING MEASUREMENTS

Today's technology could not exist without precise measurements. The science of measurement is called metrology. Metrologists are working to make sure that the world's measuring systems are accurate. In the United States, the National Institute of Standards and Technology (NIST) develops measurement standards and techniques for science and industry.
All measurements are based on a set of standard units called the System Internationale (SI). There are seven SI base units:

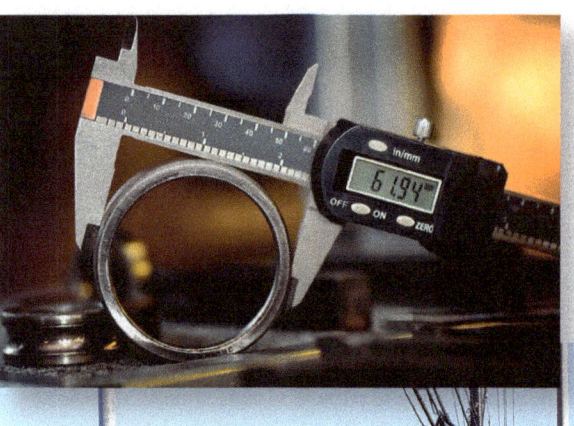

- second (time)
- meter (length)
- kilogram (mass or weight)
- ampere (electric current)
- Kelvin (temperature)
- candela (brightness)
- mole (amount)

Some of these units are familiar—you use them every day. Mole is perhaps the least well-understood. It is used for measuring the number of atoms and molecules in a substance. Other measurements, such as power, frequency, voltage, and pressure, are made by combining two or more of these base units together. For example, speed (velocity) is measured using time and length units, for example meters per second or miles per hour.

Setting standards. The SI base units have a long history. For example, the meter, the standard unit of length, was set in 1791. One meter was defined as one ten-millionth of the distance from the equator to the North Pole. The original measurements of this distance were slightly wrong, but the unit still worked just as well. The unit of mass, the kilogram (kg), was also defined from the meter. A cube of water measuring 10 centimeters (0.1 meters) on all sides was set at a mass of 1 kg. All other weights were compared to this standard.

SI Standards. In the past, metrologists created standards for the different SI units. For example, since 1889, a cylinder of platinum and iridium stored at the International Bureau of Weights and Measures (BIPM) in France served as the SI standard for a mass equal to exactly 1 kilogram. However, the mass of this cylinder changed slightly over time as it gained and lost molecules. The system works well enough for measuring everyday items. But modern technology demands precise measurement based on units that never change and can be checked at any time.

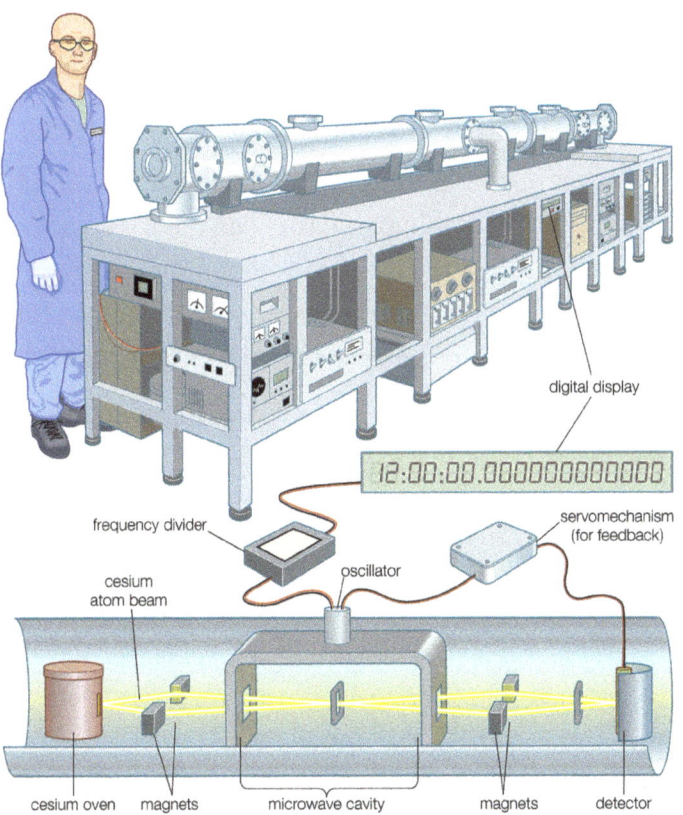

Universal constants. The modern SI units are now based on universal constants. These are units based on quantities found in nature that have an unchanging value over time. In 2018, BIPM member nations approved a new standard for the kilogram based on Planck's constant. In physics, Planck's constant is a universal fundamental measure that cannot change over time. It is a value derived from the frequency of a wave of light in relation to the energy of a photon in that wave.

The unit of time is based on the way electrons move inside a cesium atom. It takes one second for 9,192,631,770 electron jumps to occur in this atom. Metrologists are always making new measurements of these constants and others, so the SI base units and all other measurements are as precise as possible.

ENGAGE YOUR READER

Nonfiction writing often includes subject-specific vocabulary terms. Knowing the words related to the topic helps us understand the text itself.

When good readers come upon words they don't know well, they pause and try to figure them out. One tool they use is the glossary, like the one on page 4. Not every word can be defined in a glossary, though!

Authors know this, so they leave clues about words in the text. Next time you encounter a challenging word, stop and look for information about its meaning in the surrounding sentences. Sometimes authors define the term right there in the text! Other times, they'll compare the term to something you may already know. Authors even use punctuation like commas or dashes to clue you in to a word's meaning.

INSTRUCTIONS

1. Consider the list of challenge words and identify where each is used in the text. You can use the Index on page 48 to help you locate each term.

2. Explain how the author described each word. Ask yourself "what is happening in the text?" or "how is this word being used?" as you search for clues about their meanings.

3. Create your own definitions of the words. Don't just copy the dictionary definitions. Instead think about how you would tell a friend what each term means.

4. Add a visual representation for each word. Think about what you could draw that will help you remember what the words mean.

Visit www.worldbook.com/resources to download your own graphic organizer as well as other free resources!

CHALLENGE WORDS

- Nanotechnology
- Exhaust
- Composite
- Component
- Adsorption
- Ultraviolet
- Sounding
- Constant

EXAMPLE

Challenge Word	Page(s)	Author's Description	Personal Definition	Visual Representation
Nanotechnology	5, 37, 40-41	- tiny machines - devices the size of atoms - smaller than the width of a human hair - precision	Nanotechnology is a new area of technology where incredibly small devices and even machines can be built from a handful of atoms.	
Exhaust				

INDEX

A
afterburners, 8
aircraft, 5, 7, 8, 9, 10, 11, 12, 13, 15, 16, 18, 19, 20, 21, 23, 24, 29, 30, 32, 33
airliner, 18, 19
alloys, 13, 26
altimeters, 33
aluminum, 13, 39

B
bathymetry, 34, 35
biofuels, 16, 27
blades, 8, 11, 12, 13, 14, 15, 24

C
carbon dioxide, 16, 17, 30
carbon fibers, 12
chromatography, 27
climate change, 7, 16, 29
composites, 5, 12, 26
compressor, 8, 9, 10, 11, 13
crystal, 13, 41

E
eddy currents, 24
electric airplane, 20
engines, 5, 7, 8, 9, 10, 11, 12, 13, 14, 15, 16, 17, 18, 19, 20, 21, 24
Event Horizon Telescope (EHT), 43
exhaust, 8, 9

F
fuel, 5, 7, 8, 9, 10, 12, 16, 17, 18, 19, 21

G
gasoline, 16, 20
greenhouse gas, 7, 16, 30

H
helicopter, 9
hybrid engine, 21

hydrogen, 17, 18, 19, 21
hypersonic, 10, 19

I
infrared cameras, 24
International Bureau of Weights and Measures (BIPM), 45

J
jets, 7, 8, 9, 10, 11, 12, 13, 14, 15, 16, 17, 18, 19, 20

K
kerosene, 16, 17

L
Large Hadron Collider (LHC), 42
lidar, 32, 35

M
manufacturing, 5, 23, 36, 37
Massachusetts Institute of Technology (MIT), 15
mass spectrometer, 26
materials, 5, 7, 11, 12, 23, 25, 26, 27, 30, 32, 40, 41
metal, 12, 13, 14, 19, 24, 25, 26
metrology, 44
microchips, 5, 25, 37, 38, 39
microfabrication, 38, 39, 40

N
nanotechnology, 5, 37, 40, 41
National Institute of Standards and Technology (NIST), 44
nondestructive testing, 23

P
particle accelerator, 42
photolithography, 38, 39, 40
plasma thruster, 19
propeller, 9, 11, 20, 21

Q
quantum dot, 41

R
radar, 32, 33, 34
radiation, 30, 31

radiography, 25
remote sensing, 5, 29, 30, 31, 32, 34
rocket, 10, 18, 19
Rolls-Royce, 11, 20

S
satellite, 5, 29, 30, 31, 32
scatterometers, 33
scientific instruments, 5, 26, 37, 42
scramjet, 10
sensors, 5, 20, 29, 30, 32, 33
SI base units, 44, 45
silicon, 38, 39, 41
Solar Impulse, 2 21
sonar, 35
sounding, 34, 35
spectrometer, 26, 30
speed of sound, 9, 10, 19
supersonic, 8, 10, 15
sustainable aviation fuel (SAF), 16
Synergetic Air-Breathing Rocket Engine (SABRE), 18, 19

T
testing, 5, 14, 17, 22, 23, 24, 26, 27
thermal barrier, 13
thermal testing, 24
thrust, 8, 9, 10, 11, 14, 18, 19, 21
titanium, 13
turbine, 8, 9, 10, 11, 12, 13, 14, 24
turbofan, 9, 10, 11, 14, 17
turbojet, 8, 9, 19
turboprop, 9, 21
turboshaft, 9

U
ultraviolet, 30, 38, 39

W
wide-chord shape, 14, 15
wind tunnel, 14, 15

www.ingramcontent.com/pod-product-compliance
Lightning Source LLC
Chambersburg PA
CBHW041137170426
43198CB00023B/2981